THE LOWDOWN ON DENIM

TANYA LLOYD KYI

ILLUSTRATED BY CLAYTON HANMER

annick press
toronto + new york + vancouver

© 2011 Tanya Lloyd Kyi (text)
© 2011 Clayton Hanmer (illustrations)

Edited by Catherine Marjoribanks
Copy edited by Gillian Watts
Proofread by Tanya Trafford

Interior design by Grace Cheong
Cover design by theBookDesigners
Cover illustration by Clayton Hanmer

Photo credits: **denim pocket,** © iStockphoto Inc./Stuart Burford; **jeans label (small),** © Shutterstock/Sayanski; **jeans label (large),** © iStockphoto Inc./amete

Annick Press Ltd.

We acknowledge the support of the Canada Council for the Arts, the Ontario Arts Council, and the Government of Canada through the Canada Book Fund (CBF) for our publishing activities.

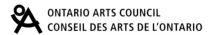

ONTARIO ARTS COUNCIL
CONSEIL DES ARTS DE L'ONTARIO

Cataloging in Publication

Kyi, Tanya Lloyd, 1973-
    The lowdown on denim / Tanya Lloyd Kyi ; illustrated by Clayton Hanmer.

Includes bibliographical references and index.
ISBN 978-1-55451-355-0 (bound).—ISBN 978-1-55451-354-3 (pbk.)

    1. Jeans (Clothing)—History—Juvenile literature. 2. Jeans (Clothing)—Juvenile literature. 3. Jeans (Clothing)—History—Comic books, strips, etc. 4. Jeans (Clothing)—Comic books, strips, etc.
I. Hanmer, Clayton, 1978- II. Title.

GT2085.K95 2011   391   C2011-902083-1

Distributed in Canada by:
Firefly Books Ltd.
66 Leek Crescent
Richmond Hill, ON
L4B 1H1

Published in the U.S.A. by:
Annick Press (U.S.) Ltd.

Distributed in the U.S.A. by:
Firefly Books (U.S.) Inc.
P.O. Box 1338
Ellicott Station
Buffalo, NY 14205

Printed in China

Visit us at: www.annickpress.com
Visit Tanya Lloyd Kyi at: www.tanyalloydkyi.com
Visit Clayton Hanmer at: www.claytonhanmer.com

For my dad, Hopalong Cassidy fan—T.K.

For Clay, my family, Fred the cat, and that favorite pair of old jeans—C.H.

Acknowledgments

The author gratefully acknowledges the assistance of Lynn Downey at Levi Strauss & Co. and Jennifer Johnson at Lee Jeans in researching the histories of those companies. Information was also provided by Tullia Marcolongo at the Maquila Solidarity Network, Lara Kimber at the Sciencenter, and Vyara Ndejuru at Parasuco Jeans. Laura Carter and Neil Kearney at the International Textile, Garment and Leather Workers' Federation offered helpful information about the garment industry and ethical shopping.

About the Author and Illustrator

Tanya Lloyd Kyi grew up in Creston, B.C., wearing skin-tight Pulse jeans, followed by acid-washed. She switched to ripped jeans and jeans with fabric side panels while studying writing at the University of Victoria. Freelance jobs in Vancouver brought a mixture of dark wash (for formal wear) and boyfriend jeans (for office work). Tanya is also the mother of two children, an achievement that involved highly uncomfortable maternity jeans. Today, she switches between low-rise and skinny jeans. Judging by the constant changes in denim styles, it will one day prove embarrassing to have this recorded in print.

Tanya is the author of more than 12 books for children and young adults, including *50 Burning Questions*, *50 Poisonous Questions*, and *50 Underwear Questions*. She has many more questions still to ask, about many other subjects.

Clayton Hanmer (aka CTON) wasn't always a fan of blue jeans. He used to be a jogging pants kinda guy, but that all changed in the eighth grade with his first pair of denim. Today, CTON only wears jeans, unless it is too hot out.

He has done many doodles for a bunch of books and a diverse gang of publications, ranging from *Owl Magazine* and *National Geographic Kids* to *The Globe and Mail* and *The New York Times*.

CONTENTS

INTRODUCTION 1

CHAPTER 1 Birth of the Blues 5

CHAPTER 2 Zip It 15

CHAPTER 3 The Wild West 23

CHAPTER 4 Wartime 33

CHAPTER 5 Rock and Revolution 43

CHAPTER 6 Freedom 53

CHAPTER 7 Black Market Blues 63

CHAPTER 8 Hair Bands and Acid Wash 73

CHAPTER 9 Street Cred 83

CHAPTER 10 Indie Labels 93

FURTHER READING 104

BIBLIOGRAPHY 104

INDEX 106

INTRODUCTION

The American denim industry makes about $13 billion each year selling all kinds of blue jeans—from affordable pairs to high-fashion versions that only the super-rich can buy. Why do shoppers spend all this money on an ordinary item of clothing?

Somehow, jeans have become pants that carry a message. Way back in the Great Depression, they represented the rugged, independent image of the cowboy. They became the preferred pant of iconic rock stars and teen rebels. Decorated in embroidery, they went to the folk concerts and peace protests of the 1970s. Today, they're everywhere: on red carpets, in factories, and in schools all over the world.

Jeans transcend nationality, politics, and social status, yet they're one of the most ordinary parts of our lives. They're all similar, and still we spend hours looking for the perfect fit and shade. And we've been wearing them for more than a century, thanks to an entrepreneur, a tailor, and a gold rush.

It all started with a man traveling on a ship bound for California …

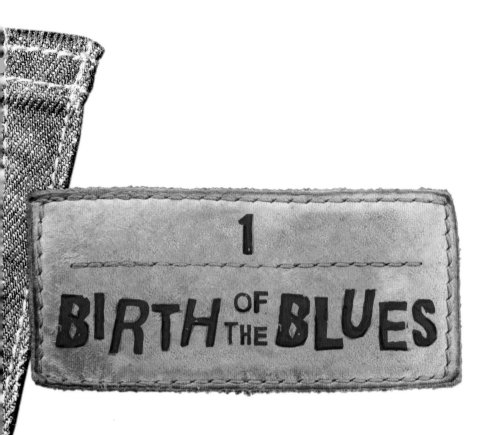

1
BIRTH OF THE BLUES

The Wild West was a promising place for a young man who wanted to get ahead. The California gold rush was on, and people were swarming through the town of San Francisco on their way to the goldfields.

Just 24 years old, Levi Strauss had come all the way from New York to make his fortune—but not by gold mining. He intended to get rich selling supplies. He opened a wholesale business that stocked clothing, canvas and other fabric, blankets, needles and thread, scissors, handkerchiefs, and pillows. Levi sold these supplies to small stores throughout California.

Heavy-duty pants were among the most popular items sold through Levi's wholesale business. Many of the hopeful prospectors were city slickers, and they needed tough work clothes for the messy business of mining.

evi's durable workpants and his other products sold so well that in 1866 he moved his business to a larger location, on busy Battery Street. To celebrate the company's success, he outfitted the new building with the leading technologies of the time: elevators and gas chandeliers.

By the time the California gold rush drew to a close in the mid-1860s, Levi was well on his way to making his fortune.

That guy had brains. He made way more cash than most of the gold miners did.

I've heard they actually do make cash from blue jeans. They take truckloads of cotton clothing and recycle it back into cotton fiber. Then they use the fiber to make paper—the strong, flexible type used to print money. It's tougher than paper made from wood fiber, so it doesn't fall apart from all the handling.

When their gold pans started coming up empty in California, Americans began to look for riches elsewhere. In the early 1870s, silver was found in Nevada—thick seams of it lying just under the ground. Soon boom towns were springing up and lucky miners were bragging of bigger and bigger bonanzas.

Inside a tailor's shop in the mining town of Reno, Jacob Davis was considering the ragged pair of workpants on the table in front of him. How could he make his pants stronger? Just that morning he'd been talking with a woman who wanted better pants for her husband to wear while chopping wood. And the miners were constantly stuffing rocks in their pockets and ripping the seams.

Jacob had done everything he could to make his denim pants tough, including ordering high-quality fabric directly from Levi Strauss in San Francisco. But the men still managed to rip their pockets. If Jacob couldn't find a solution quickly, he was going to lose his reputation as a skilled tailor.

Like Levi Strauss, Jacob was an immigrant. He had been born in Latvia, just west of Russia. And just as Levi had done 20 years before, Jacob was trying to create his own bonanza by selling clothing and equipment to miners. He just needed to make pants that wouldn't tear, no matter what.

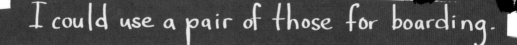

I could use a pair of those for boarding.

One day Jacob noticed the reinforced seam on a horse blanket. That was it! The strong copper rivets used for riding equipment could be used on pants as well! But what if someone stole his idea?

The oldest pair of 501 jeans still in existence dates from about 1879. The extra-crusty pants are stored in the Levi Strauss & Co. archives in San Francisco.

But Jacob didn't have the cash to patent his idea. That's where Levi came in.

Jacob turned to his main supplier for help. He wrote a letter to Levi Strauss, proposing that Levi join him in a partnership, sharing the costs and the profits from the new idea.

Today, at the head office of Levi Strauss & Co. in San Francisco, there is a typed letter titled "Transcription." Historians aren't absolutely sure it was really written by Jacob, but it sure seems authentic. It reads:

> *The secratt of them pants is the Rivits that I put in those pockets and I found demand so large that I cannot make them up fast enough. I knew you can make a very large amount of money on it if you make up pants the way I do.*

Jacob and Levi got together and got their patent, and blue jeans were born. But they still weren't called jeans. They were known as "waist-high overalls" or "waist overalls."

The new riveted pants were wildly successful. Levi invited Jacob to move to San Francisco and manage manufacturing of the waist overalls.

Jacob supervised the people who cut the fabric, then he sent the cut pieces to seamstresses who worked in their homes, sewing the pants

by hand. Other workers added the rivets, banging them through the layers of fabric with a maul—a heavy wooden hammer.

Soon the seamstresses couldn't keep up with the demand. So, instead of paying people to sew in their homes, Levi and Jacob opened new factories and hired dozens of women. But the factories were crowded, and ten-hour days were routine, six days a week. What's more, many of the workers were just teenagers.

It wasn't until the 1930s that workers were able to band together in unions and campaign for more humane treatment. Seamstresses pushed for higher wages, and slowly governments passed laws that protected workers. Under today's laws, most of the teenagers in those factories wouldn't be allowed to work full time—they would be attending school instead.

In 1890, Levi's waist overalls cost about $1.50 a pair. That would be about $30 today—enough to make Levi Strauss a rich man.

By the time Levi died in 1902 (the dude was 73), he'd saved a bundle. He even donated a bunch of cash to charity. He left Levi Strauss & Co. to his nephews—Jacob, Sigmund, Abraham, and Louis Stern. Not a bad inheritance!

These guys wanted to keep the company growing. They had just one problem—competition.

2
ZIP IT

Thanks to the patent, Levi Strauss & Co. had the exclusive rights to make its successful line of jeans. But in 1891 the patent expired, and suddenly it was open season. Other people began making their own versions of the popular pants—people such as Henry David Lee.

Lee was born in Vermont in 1849 and worked in the oil industry as a young man. Then he began to cough. His chest hurt, he found it hard to breathe, and he would wake up in the middle of the night sweating and shivering. The diagnosis: tuberculosis. His doctor told him to move to the cleaner air of the American West.

In 1889 Lee coughed his way to Salina, Kansas. There he started up the H.D. Lee Mercantile Company, the largest food supplier between Kansas City and Denver, Colorado. He soon recovered his health and the business took off. Lee began selling fabric, furniture, and stationery. Despite a massive warehouse fire and constant transportation difficulties—after all, there were no paved highways in the early 1900s—the H.D. Lee Mercantile Company soon had customers all over the West.

No paved roads means no boarding, I guess!

Lee wasn't a patient man. So when his suppliers in the eastern United States couldn't guarantee a reliable supply of work clothes for him to sell, he set up his own factory. In 1911 Lee began making jackets and dungarees—pants with pockets and a flap over the chest held up by straps over the shoulders. They were similar to what we call overalls today.

For really dirty jobs, Lee came up with the idea of stitching together a pair of pants and a long-sleeved denim shirt to make a coverall. The Lee Union-All—which united dungarees and a work shirt—was born.

The first, khaki-colored Union-Alls wouldn't win any fashion awards. They looked like the coveralls mechanics wear today: heavy-duty jumpsuits with long sleeves to protect you from dirt and scratches. Each garment had two back pockets, two side pockets, and two button-up pockets on the chest—perfect for carrying an assortment of tools.

There were a few stylish touches—a wide collar, tailored cuffs at the wrists, and rolled cuffs at the ankles—but the Union-All was mainly about practicality. No sliding, no bunching, and no getting your undershirt dirty! In 1913 it was an instant success with farmers, engineers, and industrial workers. Lee had to open three factories to keep up with the demand. Within a year, Union-Alls were also available for women and as playsuits for children.

These jeans didn't come preshrunk, like they do now. Guys who wanted a better fit would just jump into a horse trough. If you wore them wet and let them dry on your body, they'd be perfect. Preshrunk jeans weren't sold until the early 1960s.

17

The Lowdown on Denim

The First World War began in 1914, and American soldiers shipping out to Europe in 1917 were outfitted in Lee's Union-Alls—the same kind that workers wore—because they were more durable than any other kind of clothing. Brigadier General Leonard Wolf ordered thousands of the garments, asking Lee's company to supply as many pairs as it could manufacture.

Back on the home front, jeans were still in high demand as work clothing. And after the war, in 1924, the Lee Company introduced the 101 Cowboy Pant. It boasted thicker denim that could stand up to hours of friction against a saddle. The rivets were placed where they wouldn't scratch the saddle leather, and a U-shaped crotch gave a little more room for comfort while riding.

I guess war can be good for business!

When the Cowboy Pant proved successful, the Lee Company introduced new versions tailored specifically for sailors and loggers. These had suspender buttons, extra pockets for tools, and seams that were ironed flat and double-stitched to make them super-strong.

The Lee Company revolutionized jeans in 1926. It replaced the buttons with a new invention—the zipper. Back then it was called a "hookless fastener." While the fasteners had already been in use for several years on shoes and tobacco pouches, the Lee Company was the first to add them to men's jeans. To help promote the new style, the company held a contest to name the zippered pants. The winning entry was Whizit, after the sound made by the new device.

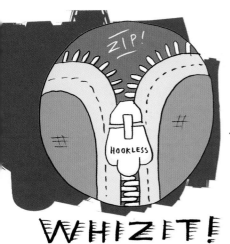

WHIZIT!

Presto … It's Open! Presto … It's Closed! Quick as a flash you can open or close the new Lee Buttonless Union-Alls, Overalls and Play Suits. Quick as a flash the whole family recognizes the comfort and convenience of these remarkable new work and play garments. The Hookless Fastener will not jam, rust or break and launders with perfect safety.

—Lee advertisement, 1927

Levi Strauss & Co. also tried some new ideas. As men's fashions changed, belt loops gradually replaced the suspender buttons on most jeans (although for several years snap-on buttons allowed men to wear suspenders if they chose). And like the Lee Company, Levi Strauss & Co. took a long look at the crotch of their pants. A small change to the design made a big difference in comfort for the country's cowboys.

Levi's jeans had a metal rivet at the base of the fly. For years, cowboys complained about it—I mean, do you really want a metal stud there when you're spending long hours in the saddle? And if you spent the evening squatting by a campfire … Ouch! The metal rivet on the crotch of your jeans could get searing hot. Designers solved the problem by getting rid of it: that rivet was history.

Jeans were getting more and more user-friendly. Soon everyone was going to want a pair!

3

THE WILD WEST

In 1929, stock markets around the world crashed. People lost their savings, businesses and banks closed, and the North American economy plunged into a dark decade now known as the Great Depression. Fifteen million Americans were out of work.

Farmers in the 1930s found that their crops were worth little, and their farms were in danger of bankruptcy. To make matters worse, a drought swept across the Great Plains and left once-fertile fields looking more like dustbowls. Now that they couldn't afford to buy new clothes every year, the farmers needed their long-lasting Levi's or Lee's more than ever.

No jobs. No crops. No skateboards. No wonder they called it "The Depression."

Times were also tough for cattle farmers. The dried-out land could no longer support massive herds, and the animals couldn't be sold for the high profits of the past. Some creative ranchers found a new source of income—tourists. Movies about the Wild West were really popular, so ranchers invited rich Americans from the East to come and experience the West. At these "dude ranches," the vacationers met real ranch hands, learned to ride the range, and dressed in the rugged style of the cowboys.

Box office phenomenon John Wayne appeared in 1930s movies dressed in boots, spurs, blue jeans, a wide silver belt buckle, a leather vest, a kerchief, and a cowboy hat. Soon that was the look everyone wanted! Tourists returning home to New York or Chicago tried to look as tough as the cowboys by wearing heeled boots and denim cowboy pants. Western clothes were even featured in the fashion magazine *Vogue*.

Jeans companies spent the 1930s emphasizing the strength of their products. In 1938 Elton Schram of Belmont, California, used a pair as a tow rope. Elton wrote Levi Strauss & Co. a letter explaining that he had found a friend stranded in his car at the side of the road. He was willing to tow his friend the 6 kilometers (4 miles) to the nearest town, but neither man had a rope. Then Elton remembered the old pair of jeans he had in his trunk. He tied one pant leg to each car and successfully rescued his friend. The pants survived without a single tear.

In 1939 Lee teamed up with *Ripley's Believe It or Not!* to create a series of advertisements celebrating the strength of Lee jeans. In one ad Ripley used a 4.5-tonne (5-ton) steamroller to iron a pair of Lee overalls. When they were peeled off the pavement, the pants were unharmed and the buttons had held their shape. In another test, one man stood in the pockets of another man's overalls without tearing the stitching.

Practically indestructible!

The Lee Company weathered the Depression by convincing workers that jeans were so strong and durable they would last twice as long as other pants. That made them a good investment! Apparently the marketing strategy worked. Lee opened a new factory in 1936 and celebrated its 50th anniversary in 1939—its Golden Jubi-Lee.

Don't look so worried.
The jeans will save you ...
just don't let go!

P eople are still doing crazy blue-jean stunts. Scientists from Cornell University and the Science Center of Ithaca once used seven pairs of jeans to lift a station wagon into the air. When the jeans survived that, the scientists lowered the car, removed one pair, and hoisted everything up again. The jeans still held. They continued removing one pair at a time until the car was dangling by a single pair. Spectators heard the threads begin to snap moments before the car tipped toward the ground. Finally the jeans gave way and ripped just above the knees.

Levi Strauss & Co. needed to set its jeans apart to outwit and outsell the competition. So Levi's designers devised ways to make their jeans immediately recognizable. They used an orange bird-wing design for the back-pocket stitching. Then, in the mid-1930s, they added a red tag to the pocket seam. The flash of red drew people's eyes, and suddenly it was easy to identify a pair of Levi's from across a room, or even across the street.

People wearing Levi's were basically carrying little company ads on their back pockets. And now tons of clothing companies do the same kind of branding—shirts have company names across the chest, shoes and hats sport logos, and sunglasses show off designer names. Practically every time we leave the house, we become walking, talking billboards for clothing brands!

In the 1940s there were only two big names in the world of jeans: Levi's and Lee. When a company called Wrangler tried to enter the market, it needed some way to convince buyers that it was a worthy brand. The company's bright idea was to use one of the most famous elements of the Wild West—the rodeo.

Ride 'em, cowboy!

Rodeos began in the American Southwest at the end of the 19th century as contests among working cowboys. These hardened horse (and bull) riders showed such skill that the events soon became popular spectator sports. Each year seemed to bring tougher competitors, able to zigzag around a course at breakneck speed and willing to risk their lives on bucking broncos. The men who won these competitions became instant heroes. Fans tried to act like them, talk like them, and dress like them. So if the Wrangler logo decorated the backsides of bull-riding, calf-tying, lasso-throwing rodeo cowboys, who wouldn't want a pair?

Wrangler hired a Philadelphia tailor named Rodeo Ben to help design and market the new cowboy pants. Already well known, Rodeo Ben had designed clothing for some of the most famous cowboys in the business. Soon all the champions were wearing Wranglers. And since men all across the West were copying the cowboy stride, the jeans got a lot of attention! So many riders across the country took to wearing Wranglers that the Professional Rodeo Cowboys Association endorsed the jeans in 1947.

Cowboys were already popular Hollywood heroes. Now the movie characters were becoming not only tough but sexy—even romantic. Gene Autry, Roy Rogers, and Hopalong Cassidy still chased villains, but sometimes they broke into song in mid-scene. And nothing made them look more like cowboys than their well-worn, snug-fitting jeans.

Gene Autry was so famous as a movie cowboy that when he joined the army in the Second World War, he was given permission to wear his cowboy boots with his uniform!

Together the Wild West heroes won thousands of fans. Women swooned over the "singing cowboys," men flocked to the movies, and kids across North America begged their parents for Western outfits. Autry, Rogers, and Cassidy all celebrated their success by releasing their own blue-jean brands.

4
WARTIME

During the Second World War, the U.S. Army needed durable clothing, and blue jeans companies were there to provide it. The clothes they made for soldiers didn't look like blue jeans, but they shared the same thick fabric and strength. Blue Bell (the company that manufactured Wrangler jeans) made 24 million items of military clothing during the war. Divided equally, that would mean that every soldier received two pieces of Blue Bell apparel. Lee also helped outfit the troops, manufacturing combat suits, flight suits, and jackets.

Wow, that's a lot of denim!

At home in North America, wartime rationing led to shortages of blue jeans. To preserve fabric and thread for the war effort, Levi's dropped extra details, including the flaps on jean jacket pockets. The bird-wing design on the back pockets of jeans wasn't absolutely necessary, so the company dropped the stitching. But rather than lose its trademark image, Levi's had the design hand-painted on every pair.

Fabric was so scarce that blue jeans were difficult to find in the stores. But the shortage seemed to make them even more popular, and wearing the hard-to-find pants became a status symbol.

Men rushed off to join the war, but who would be left to work in the factories? Countries such as Britain and Canada had a desperate need for uniforms, armor, and weaponry, but they couldn't find workers. Women came to the rescue. Some had been mothers or homemakers before the war began. Others had worked at low-paying jobs as seamstresses, secretaries, or teachers. Now they began learning trades and operating heavy machinery on the assembly lines.

Hey, JD, anything you can do, we can do, too!

In Britain in the 1930s, women were expected to stay at home. Those who did have jobs often quit when they got married. But when the war began, society changed. Everyone registered with the government, and 90 percent of single women and 80 percent of married women were asked to work for the war effort. One-third of the workers in chemical companies, metalworking industries, shipbuilding plants, and automobile factories were female.

Thousands of women also joined the workforce in Canada. When England's queen toured the country in 1939, CBC Radio broadcast her personal message to Canadian women: "We, no less than men, have real and vital work to do for our country in its hour of need."

Skirts and pumps were hardly practical for the assembly line. In 1943 the *Saturday Evening Post* published a cover story about women joining the workforce, and the famous artist Norman Rockwell painted a portrait of a working woman—"Rosie the Riveter"—holding her power tools. She wore safety goggles, rolled-up sleeves, and … denim coveralls. Soon Rosie became a symbol for working women, as well as a household name. And slacks or coveralls and bandanas became the patriotic wartime dress code.

If Rosie lived today, she'd be a boarder. No question.

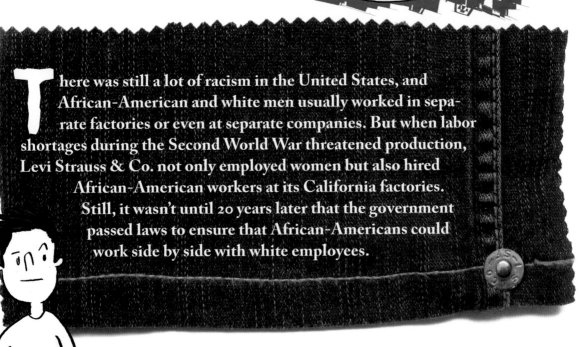

There was still a lot of racism in the United States, and African-American and white men usually worked in separate factories or even at separate companies. But when labor shortages during the Second World War threatened production, Levi Strauss & Co. not only employed women but also hired African-American workers at its California factories. Still, it wasn't until 20 years later that the government passed laws to ensure that African-Americans could work side by side with white employees.

The Lowdown on Denim

American soldiers who were lucky enough to own blue jeans during the war years often carried their favorite pairs with them to training camps and overseas. Some even managed to keep their jeans with them through the entire war. As the fighting drew to a close, soldiers would motorcycle through the European countryside wearing Levi's, or sample Paris nightlife in their Wranglers.

The people of Europe had suffered through years of food and clothing shortages, and now they were celebrating their freedom. The North American soldiers who had fought in the war were treated like heroes, and everything about them became popular—including their blue jeans.

Levi's created the first women's jeans in 1934, but they were sold almost exclusively to ranchers and farmers in the American West. Then sales increased as dude ranch visits grew popular. As the Second World War ended, Levi's began marketing jeans directly to women in all parts of the continent.

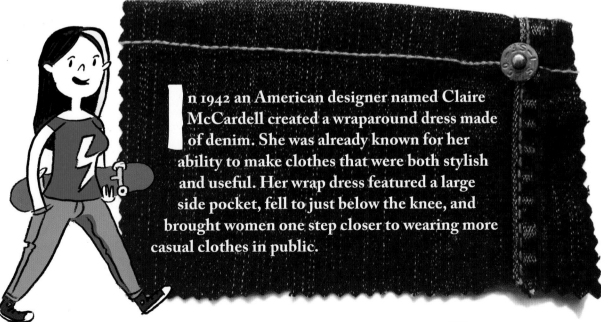

In 1942 an American designer named Claire McCardell created a wraparound dress made of denim. She was already known for her ability to make clothes that were both stylish and useful. Her wrap dress featured a large side pocket, fell to just below the knee, and brought women one step closer to wearing more casual clothes in public.

Other companies soon followed. The Blue Bell Company called its new pants "Jeanies." Advertisements proclaimed: "Jeanies for Girls. The perfect garments for work and play." Similar ads from Lee promised: "Yes-siree, these Lee Frontier Lady Pants are tailored, tapered, and trim!"

Yes-siree, they zip up the side!

Women's jeans included small design changes intended to make the pants more feminine. One company sewed the selvage seams—where the fabric is stitched so it won't fray—with pink thread instead of red.

It was Rodeo Ben, the celebrity designer hired by Wrangler, who first created jeans for women with a front zipper. That was in the late 1940s, but the new style wasn't popular right away—customers preferred the usual side zipper. It wasn't until the 1950s that a front zipper on women's pants caught on. Soon after that, jeans really began to belong everywhere, on everyone!

5
ROCK AND REVOLUTION

A lot of things changed after the war. Earlier generations of kids finished school early and then worked on the family farm or found jobs—or signed up for the army. But in the 1950s, economies were booming, so kids were staying in school longer. They often put off work and marriage so they could go to college. They came to be recognized as a whole new age group—teenagers. Teenagers were dancing to rock and roll music or living the bohemian lifestyle of beatniks, hitchhiking across the country and writing poetry. Most of all, they were making their own fashion choices. These teens weren't interested in looking like grown-ups, and they didn't want the coveralls worn by their fathers and grandfathers. They wanted style, and that included pants that fit snugly around the waist.

Denim companies rushed to meet the demand. By 1947 Wrangler's advertising slogan had changed from "The World's Largest Producer of Work Clothes" to "The World's Largest Producer of Work and Play Clothes." Meanwhile, Levi Strauss & Co. introduced 501 Shrink-to-Fits. When the wearer took a bath in them, these jeans shrank to become skintight … and sexy. They became the perfect pants for a night on the town, but they were still considered more acceptable for men than for women.

Just as cowboys helped give jeans tough, rugged appeal in the 1930s and '40s, movie stars now gave jeans glamour. In 1953 Marlon Brando starred in a film called *The Wild One*. As the leader of the Black Rebels motorcycle gang, Brando was a slick, dark figure in a leather jacket, white T-shirt, and jeans. When a girl asks, "What are you rebelling against?" the tough hipster replies, "Whaddaya got?"

The Wild One celebrated teenage rebellion and violence—so much violence that it was banned in Britain until 1968. But it sparked a trend for rebel heroes, and James Dean was the perfect next candidate. With his dark blond hair, good looks, and intense eyes, he was an immediate teen idol.

Now that was a guy with style.

Hey, JD, the 1950s called. They want their hair cream back.

In his second film, *Rebel Without a Cause,* Dean plays a "bad boy from a good family," knife-fighting with his enemies and "playing chicken" as he races his car toward a cliff, only to swerve at the last possible moment. Like Brando, Dean played it cool in white T-shirts and jeans.

In real life, James Dean loved speed. As his career caught fire, he bought a racehorse, a motorcycle, and a Porsche sports car. Shortly before the premiere of *Rebel Without a Cause,* Dean crashed his Porsche and died instantly, cementing his reputation as the ultimate bad boy.

While young men had Marlon Brando and James Dean to admire, women had Marilyn Monroe. The blonde bombshell became the ultimate sex symbol of the 1950s after starring in movies such as *Gentlemen Prefer Blondes* and *How to Marry a Millionaire*. When she began turning up at parties and in press photos wearing blue jeans that hugged her hips and showed off her curves, everyone could see that jeans could look sexy on women too, not just on men.

To young people, jeans had been the pants their dads wore to work. They were tough, but they were also baggy and worn. Movie stars such as Marlon Brando, James Dean, and Marilyn Monroe transformed the image of denim. It wasn't just for factory workers anymore. Now jeans were something you would wear while hanging out with friends on Saturday night. You might even wear them on a date.

You know why I like Marilyn Monroe? Because back when she was still Norma Jeane Baker, before she hit the big time, she pitched in during the Second World War labor shortage. She worked at the Radioplane munitions factory in Burbank, California. That's where she was "discovered" by a photographer who convinced her to try modeling … which ultimately led to a career on the big screen!

The generation gap...

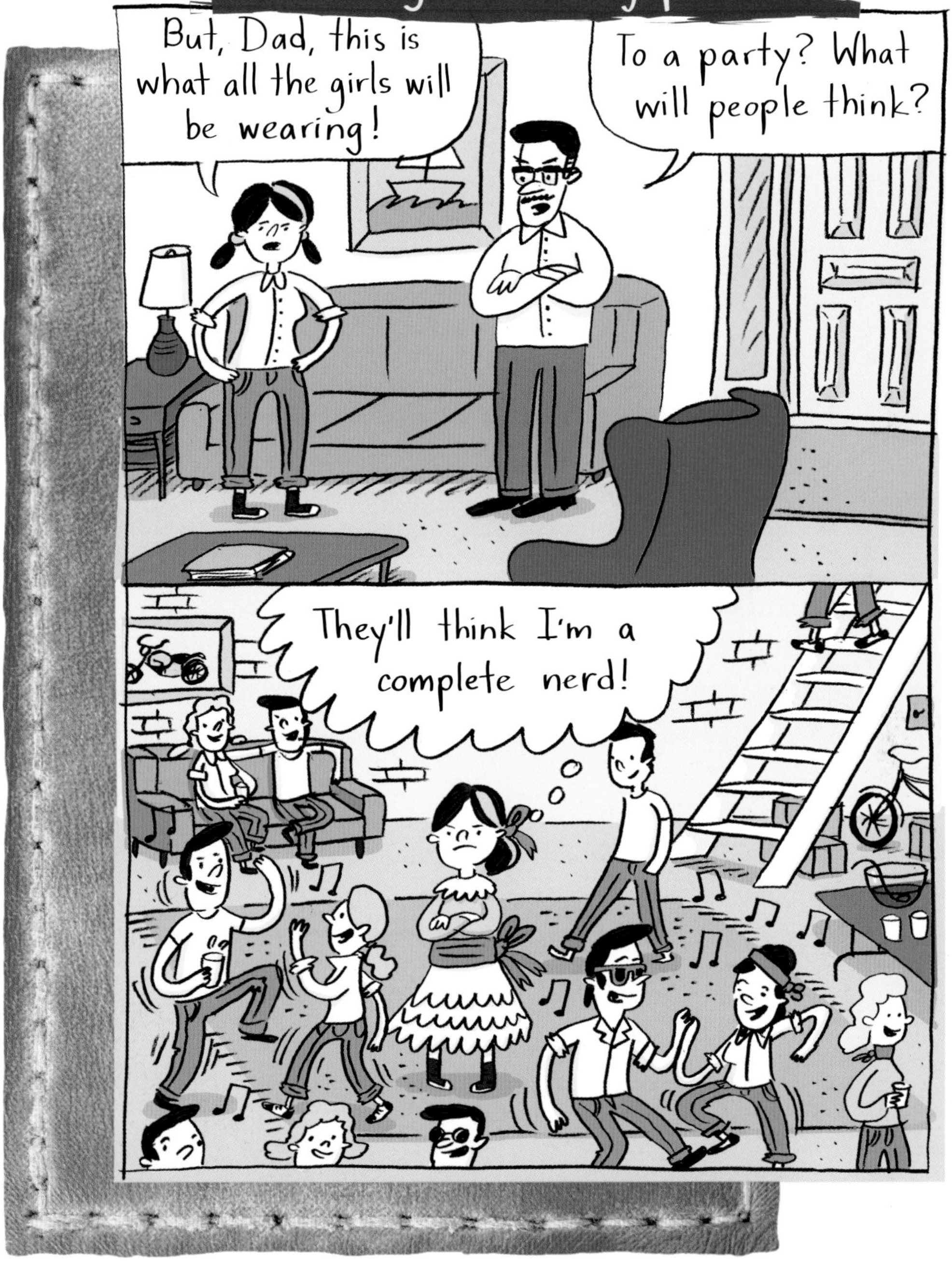

Jeans showed off their sex appeal in Europe, too. Brigitte Bardot was a French movie star in the 1950s and '60s, and many of her films showed daring glimpses of skin. Then she would slip on jeans for press appearances or star-studded parties. Instantly, denim left its factory reputation behind and became the newest sexy trend.

The 1950s brought dramatic scientific changes to the world. The Soviet Union launched Sputnik, the first man-made satellite, into space. American researcher Jonas Salk invented a vaccine to prevent polio, and the first laser was unveiled. Many 1950s inventions seemed to celebrate the social life and sense of fun of Americans: the telephone answering machine, the hula hoop, Mr. Potato Head. The same relaxed attitudes that inspired these inventions influenced more and more young people to pull on blue jeans.

Meanwhile, television was bringing news and pop culture right into people's homes. In living rooms, diners, and dance clubs, young people were jiving to the first rock and roll songs. Elvis Presley emerged as a star, crooning his way into teenage hearts as he wiggled his blue-jeans-clad hips.

I bet those blue jeans looked good with blue suede shoes, too!

Parents began worrying that young people were running wild. Were their sweet, innocent daughters being corrupted by television and movies? Could boys in tight pants and fast cars really be trusted? To parents who had lived through a depression and a war, these fun-loving young people seemed out of control.

In the 1950s movie *Blue Denim,* the blue-jeans-wearing main character is a teenage girl who is pregnant and unmarried. There are also motorcycle-riding, denim-wearing gang members. Would teenagers who wore jeans turn into juvenile delinquents? After decades of thinking of jeans as work clothes suitable for the fields or the factory, parents had trouble adjusting to the idea of jeans in high school hallways.

School principals across the United States decided they had to ban jeans.

Some schools even handed out brochures or showed short films that illustrated appropriate dress for school (below-the-knee skirts for girls, dress pants for boys, blazers and dress shirts for everyone) and inappropriate clothing choices (mainly jeans). In Britain, a vicar banned jeans in his church youth group, claiming that anyone who wore jeans was a person whose morals were "practically non-existent."

Levi Strauss & Co. reacted with a 1957 advertisement intended to convince parents and teachers that jeans were okay. In the ad, a clean-cut young man wearing jeans, a button-down shirt, and loafers carries an armload of books toward classes. Above the photo blaze the words "Right for School."

Boy, our principal would be *thrilled* if we came to school dressed like that!

The company immediately received irate letters from parents. One mother from Hillsdale, New Jersey, wrote that the kind of behavior shown in the ad might be acceptable in the West, but it certainly wasn't appropriate in the East. She felt that school was serious, and denim was much too casual. "I refer," she wrote, "to the picture showing a young boy dressed in shirt sleeves, sloppily opened at the collar and wearing dungarees…" Of course, all the debate about whether or not jeans were appropriate only made them more popular with teens.

The question of where jeans could or should be worn affected adult women as well. In 1954 a U.S. Army colonel in Germany asked the soldiers' wives to stop wearing jeans, telling them it gave Americans a poor image. He believed the Europeans would think the women were being too casual, or even too sexy. In his mind, jeans just weren't appropriate for modest married women.

In 1951, superstar singer Bing Crosby arrived at a Canadian hotel in Levi's jeans and a denim jacket. The hotel refused to allow him inside. When Levi Strauss & Co. learned of the incident, it produced a tuxedo jacket tailored specifically for Crosby—and made entirely of denim.

Jeans began as tough-as-nails work pants, then became western gear, went to war and into the factories, made it to Hollywood parties and to school … Now maybe jeans were ready to make a social statement, too.

6
FREEDOM

There was no stopping the growing popularity of jeans. From students and music fans to hippies and protesters, everyone was wearing them. They were becoming such a visible part of North American culture that the Smithsonian Institution, the world's largest museum, added jeans to its collection in 1964. And so many teens were in love with their jeans that schools and parents were eventually forced to accept them.

After all, there were more kids than ever before.

Man, our grandparents were baby-makin' machines! Between the mid-1940s and the mid-1960s, about 76 million children were born in the U.S. In 1957 a baby was born every seven seconds. In Britain the baby boom generation numbered more than 18 million, and in Canada the birth rate jumped by almost 20 percent.

By the 1960s, some of these postwar kids were starting to grow up. *Newsweek* magazine ran a feature article in 1963 called "The Teenagers: A *Newsweek* Survey of What They're Really Like." The magazine's cover showed a young girl wearing Wranglers, posing on the back of a motorcycle.

According to the article, there were 18 million teenagers in the United States, and 76 percent of them liked to shop. Girls were spending $2 billion a year on clothes. That information caught the attention of the country's blue jeans makers. It was time to promote jeans as fun, stylish, and young. Billions of dollars in profit depended on it.

Wow, if we were spending $2 billion a year way back then, I wonder what we spend now ...

But jeans companies weren't able to control trends and social patterns—they simply tried to reflect whatever values young people adopted. And in the 1960s, young people were calling for peace and love. From New York's Greenwich Village and San Francisco's Haight-Ashbury neighborhood, the hippie movement grew and spread across the country, and even around the world. Many hippies believed in pacifism, democracy, and the value of reconnecting with the earth—which included eating natural foods and wearing natural fabrics such as cotton. Blue jeans with flared legs, known as bell-bottoms, were a big feature of the hippie look.

So the hippies were antiwar and the hippies wore bell-bottoms. That's all a little ironic, considering that bell-bottoms originally came from navy uniforms. Apparently sailors liked wide-legged pants because if they fell overboard, it was easy to strip them off over their boots.

In the late 1960s and early 1970s, hippies protested the Vietnam War. Young people were rebelling against the American government, their parents, and anything else that seemed old-fashioned. These new activists took the 1950s bad-boy image of jeans and went a step further,

wearing denim as a way of rejecting their parents' lifestyle. Marshall McLuhan, a writer who specialized in exploring North American culture, said, "Jeans represent a ripoff and a rage against the establishment."

Jeans were now firmly established as clothing for everyday life. They'd come a long way from the Wild West ranches, and they were no longer reserved for weekends and evenings—no matter what parents said or how much grandparents complained. Because teens were wearing them everywhere, jeans became more socially acceptable. At Woodstock, a huge outdoor concert in 1969 that drew more than half a million young people and antiwar protesters, it seemed as though everyone was wearing jeans. There were only two ways to look cool at Woodstock: wear your jeans or go naked.

To teens, the era was all about freedom—freedom to live differently and think differently from your parents, and freedom to express yourself through your clothing. Gradually jeans became a great social leveler. No matter what your color, gender, or social class, you could still wear a cool pair of hip-huggers.

Having your own style was one way to prove that you were unique, so teens began altering or individualizing their jeans. Some embroidered the denim with flowers, some painted on peace symbols, some tie-dyed the fabric, and others cut open the seams and inserted colorful cotton strips.

It didn't take long for the marketing departments of jeans companies to see the potential in decorated jeans. Soon factories were mass-producing jeans with fancy stitching and patterns and patches. Meanwhile, teens were recycling their blues into denim patchwork pants, cut-off shorts, shoulder bags, and miniskirts.

The world was changing quickly, and jeans were changing just as fast. In only a generation, blue jeans had gone from safe to psychedelic; they'd transformed into a hip, rebellious choice for teens. Where would they go next?

Of course, if you wanted to make absolutely sure you were hip to the latest trends, you could check out what your favorite musicians were wearing. Sonny and Cher helped make bell-bottoms famous, and the Rolling Stones rocked it in hip-huggers.

Mods vs. Rockers...

BATTLE OF THE BANDS

By the 1970s, you could almost tell teens' musical taste by their choice of pants. Rock and rollers wore blue jeans with low waistbands and wide belts. The modernists—known as "Mods"—were taking their cue from 1960s pop bands, wearing tailored suits and pointy shoes. And those stayin' alive on the American disco scene had ditched their jeans in favor of polyester pants, colorful button-up shirts, and platform shoes. Someone truly stylish might don a polyester pant-and-jacket combination known as the "leisure suit."

Hey, man, this look is killin' me. Gimme my jeans back!

With all the changes going on—from personalized hippie style to funky disco looks and tough-guy rockers—you might think the jeans companies would have trouble keeping up. Well, they did expand their focus a little. For example, Lee introduced LEEsures, and Levi Strauss & Co. expanded its line to include polyester patterned pants, although they still had bell bottoms. The ads proclaimed: "Dull has gone out of style."

But even with this influx of new fabrics and styles, blue jeans were experiencing a golden age of popularity.

7
BLACK MARKET BLUES

The teen rebels of the late 1970s and early 1980s made James Dean look angelic in comparison. Punks, as they called themselves, didn't rebel just against school uniforms or government policies. They set themselves against all of society—the entire establishment. Symbolized by bands such as New York's The Ramones and London's The Clash, punks were ready to declare a rule of anarchy—in life and in fashion.

It was time to *deconstruct* clothing. Punks believed in bucking the rules of the middle class. If Mom and Dad thought hair should be neatly brushed, then punks wanted to dye theirs pink and green and shave it into mohawks. And if the uptight next-door neighbors thought clothing should be clean and neat, then punks wanted to rip, shred, and fray their jeans. If the pants had to be held together with safety pins, that was even better.

The Lowdown on Denim

As Sid Vicious and the Sex Pistols screamed their way onto the punk stage, they symbolized a new direction—in music and in denim. For the first time, jean trends weren't flowing from North America toward the rest of the world. Some of these ideas were originating in Britain and the rest of Europe, and spreading back to the United States.

Now we're thinking globally!

European and Asian teens had been wearing blue jeans ever since the Second World War ended and the soldiers left some of their gear behind. A few decades later, sales around the world were booming. For American companies, this worldwide love affair with denim was a dream come true. Millions of international consumers were clamoring to buy jeans, and Europe's clothing companies were lagging behind.

The Lee Company moved more quickly, opening an international division in New York City and its first overseas operation, a factory in Belgium. By the end of the 1960s, Lee jeans were being sold in Scotland, Spain, Australia, Brazil, and Hong Kong.

Levi Strauss & Co. wasn't far behind, exhibiting at a Paris show in 1961, creating Levi Strauss International in 1965, and opening Levi Strauss Japan in 1971. Wrangler jeans hit the world market in 1962, when the company also opened a plant in Belgium.

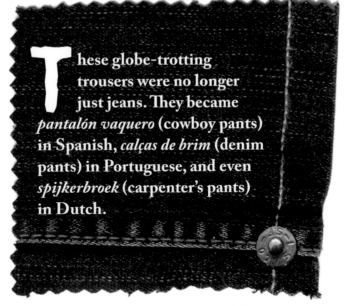

These globe-trotting trousers were no longer just jeans. They became *pantalón vaquero* (cowboy pants) in Spanish, *calças de brim* (denim pants) in Portuguese, and even *spijkerbroek* (carpenter's pants) in Dutch.

Denim companies were busily expanding around the world, but they weren't welcome in every country. In communist countries such as the USSR, government officials saw blue jeans as a corrupting force. They believed that buying Western goods such as jeans and rock music records would lure young people away from communism and toward capitalism. They also believed that popular culture promoted poor morals—tight-fitting jeans were one more symbol of American corruption.

Tight jeans? Uncomfortable maybe. Evil? Not so sure about that!

Government disapproval didn't prevent people in communist countries from wanting jeans, though. In 1979 a tourist in Moscow wandered the unfamiliar streets until he found a café where he could take a break. He was thrilled when a few Russian men introduced themselves and sat down to chat. Soon they were sharing a bottle of vodka. They had two drinks, then three, then four, then … Wait—how did he end up outside? Where was his hotel? And … where were his pants?! This time the traveler found himself wandering the streets dressed only in his underwear.

The story may sound far-fetched, but it's exactly what happened to a Norwegian tourist. His new Russian "friends" turned out to be interested only in his blue jeans.

In 1946 British politician Winston Churchill said, "From Stettin in the Baltic to Trieste in the Adriatic, an iron curtain has descended across the continent." He meant that the communist countries had isolated their citizens by restricting trade, censoring the news, and limiting travel. Behind this Iron Curtain, European young people were just like us. They yearned for things such as rock music, blue jeans, and fast-food hamburgers. To many of them, American popular culture represented freedom.

When communist governments locked the front door, blue jeans snuck in through the back. Smugglers made thousands of dollars bringing denim across closed borders. In Russia a single pair could sell for a month's wages. In Yugoslavia in 1977, police arrested bootleggers trying to bring 1,200 pairs of jeans into the country—jeans that might have sold for up to $100 a pair if they had made it to the streets.

Smuggling was also successful on a smaller scale. Western tourists on vacation in Russia could help fund their trips by taking along a few extra pairs of Levi's. Some experts believe that in the late 1970s, about 10,000 pairs of jeans a year were secretly imported by black marketers, while another 100,000 pairs arrived in the country with tourists, foreign students, and businesspeople.

Vacationers who weren't willing to part with their pants might find that Russian young people could be less than friendly. The young Norwegian who was robbed of his jeans in Moscow wasn't the only traveler to find himself in trouble. In one Soviet city, members of a youth league chased a man through the streets and demanded his pants.

When he refused to hand them over, he was stabbed. In another incident, teenage girls used knives and razor blades to attack two people and steal their jeans.

Yikes! I love my jeans, but I wouldn't risk my life for them!

Unable to stop illegal blue jeans from flowing across the border, East German officials decided on a different strategy—they would try to make money from the trend. After all, if jeans could sell for so much on the black market, why shouldn't the government get a share of the profit?

In 1978 the East German government ordered 800,000 pairs of jeans from Levi Strauss & Co. The pants were flown across the border and East German young people lined up at store counters across the country, hoping to get the "real thing." Each shopper was allowed to buy one pair for the equivalent of more than $70. Since the government had purchased the pants for $11.25 a pair, there was plenty of profit to be made.

In Hungary, the communist government was more flexible about importing jeans to meet demands. In 1977 a million pairs were sold through stores. Eventually four Hungarian companies negotiated with Levi Strauss & Co. for permission to produce jeans for the Eastern European market. The jeans were on store shelves by 1979, bearing the all-important Levi's label on the back pockets.

Why were jeans so popular? Not only were they a symbol of Western freedom, they were a sign of wealth and power in communist society. People who wore jeans had traveled overseas, they had access to the American cash needed to buy black-market goods, or they had rich and influential friends.

The Lowdown on Denim

Wrangler set up factories in Europe to meet the increased demand. In 1983 the first Original Levi's Store opened in Spain, and hundreds more followed in countries from Germany to Japan. In fact, Levi's were so popular in Germany that the company won the German Apparel Supplier of the Year award in 1990—the first non-German company to win.

Meanwhile, a few European companies had been producing their own versions of blue jeans. After all, the patent on riveted pants had expired way back in 1891, and there was nothing to stop companies around the world from trying to capture a piece of the market. But while some European designs—including tight-fitting styles—were popular, it was decades before a brand other than Levi's, Lee, or Wrangler really cashed in.

In 1991 a Turkish textile company launched its own label—Mavi Jeans—in Istanbul (*mavi* means "blue" in Turkish). Within three years Mavi was selling jeans throughout Europe, and by 1998 it was exporting a million pairs a year to customers from Canada to Croatia.

In 2003 Mavi was the second-most recognized brand name in Turkey, second only to Coca-Cola.

Now jeans were in demand all over the world. But once everyone had a pair or two, how could the manufacturers get them to buy more?

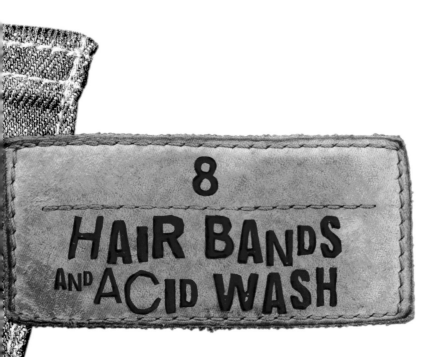

8
HAIR BANDS
AND ACID WASH

Music in the late 1970s and early '80s embraced everything from heavy metal to New Wave to punk to glam rock, and jeans showed up everywhere—ripped and dirty or blinged up and pristine.

Denim had already been immortalized in songs such as the 1956 release "The Blue Jean Bop." When Neil Diamond sang "Forever in Blue Jeans" in 1978, it topped the charts.

Andy Warhol was an artist famous in the 1970s for painting

In 1977 a member of the Texas legislature actually proposed that jeans be declared the official state garment.

seemingly ordinary bits of North American culture. In the decade before, he had painted a Campbell's soup can, bottles of Coca-Cola, and portraits of celebrities such as Marilyn Monroe. In 1971 the Rolling Stones asked Warhol to design a cover for their newest

album, *Sticky Fingers*. Warhol's creation featured a photograph of jeans, and attached to the image was a real working zipper. In the 1980s, Bruce Springsteen released the album *Born in the U.S.A.*—its cover featuring his rear, clad in denim.

In 1979 a clothing maker, the Murjani Corporation, approached Gloria Vanderbilt, a famous heiress, artist, and clothing designer. The company proposed that Gloria lend her name to a new line of blue jeans. Tight-fitting and bearing her signature on the back pocket, Gloria Vanderbilt jeans were a hit and introduced a whole new world of upscale "designer" denim.

Inspired by this new, tight-fitting style, a company called Jordache pioneered the "Jordache look" of sexy denim in the late 1970s. Meanwhile, Calvin Klein had also gone into the jeans business, and his company was raising eyebrows with ads featuring teen star Brooke Shields. She sashayed onto the TV screen and purred, "You know what comes between me and my Calvins? Nothing"—implying that she wasn't wearing any underwear.

In magazine ads that appeared at the same time, Shields was shown posing in tight jeans and unbuttoning her shirt. The ads sparked concern not only because they were so openly sexual but also because Shields was only 15 years old. Critics accused Calvin Klein of exploiting a young girl, and some even called the ads child pornography. CBS and other TV stations banned the commercials, but the move only brought Calvin Klein more publicity. His ads may have been controversial, but they were hugely successful.

Calvin Klein had started a trend: clothing models were stripping off the layers. Soon rap star Marky Mark was posing in his boxer shorts and Claudia Schiffer was dancing in her Victoria's Secret underwear. Today we see semi-naked models on billboards whenever we drive through city streets. Sex sells.

Getting on the brand wagon...

So what's the big thing I had to come down here to see?

I told you my jeans would make me famous some day!

WINK

JD
BRAND JEANS

Not you, too, JD!

Using sex appeal wasn't the only way that jeans companies tried to distinguish their brands. French designers Marithe and François Girbaud, for example, noticed that jeans were most loved once they'd been worn a few times and had lost their "new blue" look. The couple set out to find the perfect process for pre-aging denim. They destroyed a few industrial-sized washing machines along the way.

Check out what these two tried, looking for the perfect method:

1. Washing denim with sand. Messy.
2. Washing denim with large rocks. Destroyed machines. Expensive.
3. Washing denim with pumice stone, a lava rock that floats. Success!

The "stonewashed" look was born!

Stonewashed jeans proved so popular throughout the 1980s that other companies developed their own versions. The Lee Company tried washing its denim with shredded rubber tires, bottle caps, golf balls, rope, and wood chips before finally settling on pumice stone as well. At the height of the stone-washed craze, Lee employed 10,000 people at 17 sewing plants and five laundries, and they could produce 200,000 pairs of jeans every day. At one point the company was spending $2 million a year buying rocks!

I think they must have had rocks in their heads!

Other companies used bleach to wear down their denim. Manufacturers in Italy and the United States simultaneously developed a method of soaking pumice stones in bleach, then adding them to a dryer full of denim to create random bleach spots, a look they called "acid-washed."

Not every company tried to reinvent denim. When Ralph Lauren added jeans to his Polo clothing line in 1978, he paired the denim with leather vests and jackets, patterned skirts, and fringed buckskin to celebrate cowboy history. Fashion critics loved the look, writing that he had "recaptured America for America." Ralph Lauren was so pleased with the new line that he appeared in the ads himself, dressed as if for the Wild West.

The new Polo denim appealed to older shoppers, but young people weren't interested in remembering cowboy days. The youth rebellions of the 1960s and the punk music groups of the 1970s still lived on in spirit. Many teens found that wearing ripped jeans was the perfect way to express their rebellious side—and annoy parents and teachers in the process.

By the 1980s, ripped jeans had gone from a punk phenomenon to a teen trend, and jeans companies began to take notice. Marithe and François Girbaud were the first designers to intentionally rip their new denim, calling their pre-ripped pants "destroyed jeans." Other companies

The Lowdown on Denim

followed the fad. An American firm called Jou Jou took its backlog of plain, boring styles and started ripping them—the jeans soon sold out.

Jeans had once been one-shape-fits-all garments, meant to last forever. Farm workers had never stood in changing rooms gazing into three-way mirrors and asking, "Do these pants make my butt look big?" When their old ones wore out, they simply bought a new pair, which looked almost exactly like the pair they had bought the decade before.

The introduction of designer denim changed the market. Now there was a different style for every body type and a new look with each new season. All this change left designers looking for inspiration. In 1987 Salvatore Parasuco of Parasuco Jeans hired someone to sandblast the company logo on the door of his office. He wondered aloud if the sandblasting machine could be used on jeans.

"Are you crazy?" the worker asked.

Maybe Salvatore *was* a little off kilter—he rented a sandblasting machine and tried it himself. When he sent the results to the laundry, he told people that the fabric was new and imported directly from Italy. He didn't want anyone stealing his sandblasting idea. The jeans sold for $65 a pair and were just one of the chic designs that led to Parasuco's opening showrooms in Montreal, New York, Los Angeles, and Milan.

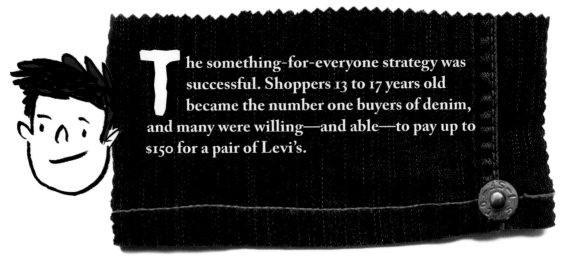

The something-for-everyone strategy was successful. Shoppers 13 to 17 years old became the number one buyers of denim, and many were willing—and able—to pay up to $150 for a pair of Levi's.

By the 1990s there were hundreds of jeans variations: tight, baggy, dark, faded, boot-cut, bell-bottomed, and beaded. There was a different pair for everyone's taste and budget—especially if that budget happened to be huge. A Roberto Cavalli design with a beaded waistband went for a whopping $1,840. Gucci jeans with torn knees were showcased on fashion runways in 1999, and they sold out instantly. They cost $3,715 a pair.

In Vancouver, a designer named Jason Dussault created Trashed Denim—hand-painted jeans encrusted with gold. They sold for $250,000 a pair.

9

STREET CRED

By the late 1980s, fresh new music was coming up from the clubs. Hip hop and rap were reaching a mainstream audience. And with the new sound came a new fashion. Jeans, worn low and baggy, were bad-boy again. And some of them were being sewn by the bad boys themselves.

In 1989 the American government had seized the profits of some drug-smuggling operations and was looking for a good way to spend the cash. Meanwhile, the state of Oregon was looking for a way to make its prisons less expensive—feeding all those convicts was costing a bundle. State officials decided that, with a federal grant, they could start a prison sewing department. So in 1989, prisoners at the Eastern Oregon Correction Institution started making uniforms and blue jeans for inmates. Prisoners could sign up for jobs at the production facility. After the government had taken back some cash for prison costs and taxes, the men were allowed to spend their wages or send the money to their families.

Then, in 1997, the jailhouse expanded operations and started marketing its Prison Blues line outside the prison—to regular everyday shoppers. The jeans were sold under the motto "Made on the Inside to be Worn on the Outside."

Do you suppose they look like the jeans Elvis was wearing in *Jailhouse Rock*?

Something similar happened in Europe. At Berlin's Tegel Prison, prisoners had been sewing their own uniforms since the 1800s, and other clothes they made were being sold through a small shop nearby. For years, the salespeople there would smile innocently at shoppers and tell them, "These clothes are made by local craftspeople," or "The sewers come from different backgrounds." Basically they did everything possible to avoid telling the truth: the clothes were made by convicts.

But in 2003 a Berlin advertising agency convinced the prison to change its approach. The agency launched a website and labeled shoes, briefcases, and denim jackets with the brand name Haeftling, which means "inmate" in German. Within two weeks, the prison had received 3,000 orders.

Ever since the days of James Dean, blue jean companies had promoted a bad-boy image as a way to increase sales. Jeans could make you look tough. So jeans made in prison, by prisoners, in the same style as worn by prisoners—that was just taking the image one step further.

Jailhouse fashion had already sparked another trend. Because prisoners weren't allowed to have belts (or anything else that could be used to hurt themselves or others), they wore their jeans loose around the hips. The style was soon picked up by urban teens as a fashion dubbed "saggin'."

Saggin' jeans sparked big controversy. Several cities and towns in the United States even banned the style. Because men wearing low-slung jeans expose a strip of underwear above their waistband, some city councils called it "indecent exposure" or "disorderly conduct"—even if no skin was showing.

The Lowdown on Denim

The American Civil Liberties Union protested these laws, claiming they unfairly targeted African-Americans. After all, it was young black males in urban centers who were most likely to wear the style. President Obama even talked about the issue during an MTV appearance. He said kids should pull up their pants, but also that public officials who were spending their time worrying about saggin'—they should focus on real problems instead.

In Europe, low-rise jeans hit the fashion headlines thanks to Alexander McQueen, a designer known for clothing both shocking and political. He launched his "bumsters" in 1996, sending models down the catwalk with their butt cracks showing.

Oh, sorry, but that's seriously TMI!

The pants were a hit. Young people eagerly adopted the style, and one year after he released the collection, 27-year-old McQueen was named the head designer at Givenchy in Paris.

While men were copying the styles of hip-hop artists, women were adopting their own street-worthy fashions, including low-rise hip-huggers that revealed the waistband of their underwear. "Boyfriend jeans" were loose and baggy, made to look as if the girl had borrowed her guy's pants. They were worn with tight, midriff-baring tops.

In North America, the saggin' style was popularized by some big-name rap stars. For many rappers, success depended on a bad-boy reputation: they had to look as if they'd done hard time in prison (and a few of them had). Their baggy, low-rise jeans were a part of that image.

As television and music videos took rap and hip hop from the inner cities to the suburbs, the fashion traveled, too. In the early 1990s, hip hop–inspired styles were available only in a few big-city stores. Then music stars such as Russell Simmons and Sean (Diddy) Combs started

their own lines of menswear, and low-rise jeans and oversized shirts became available in every North American mall. Meanwhile, teen pop stars such as Britney Spears popularized the low-rise style for women.

As hip hop grew more and more popular, some people started noticing how many brand-name and designer products appeared in the videos. There were shots of designer jeans, watches, cars, and running shoes. Were the companies paying to have their brands associated with the tough image of the hip-hop artists? The musicians insisted they weren't accepting money, but a few companies confessed to product-placement plans. The truth? The people who know aren't telling.

Always watching out for new trends, Levi Strauss & Co. released its Dangerously Low line of jeans for men. Diesel Jeans also produced men's hip-huggers, and the company snagged a huge publicity boost when Brad Pitt started wearing his to Hollywood events.

Jeans were more popular than ever. Or were they? Teen buyers still kept an eye out for the latest denim trends, but they had other issues on their minds as well—issues such as globalization and fair trade. At the end of the twentieth century, some people began looking at jeans from a different angle, and they didn't always like what they were finding below the belt.

10
INDIE LABELS

With the advent of file sharing and YouTube, music lovers can load their MP3 players with unique and individual mixes. They can also use social networking sites to launch and promote their own independent music careers.

And that creative spirit applies to fashion, too. When looking for jeans, twenty-first-century shoppers can choose organic cotton, fair-trade brands, even form-fitting pairs that can be worn for six months without a wash. You can't get more personalized than that!

Increasingly, shoppers' jean choices are political as well as personal. Until the 1990s, most teens never stopped to think about who had sewn their jeans and whether the companies that sold them were good corporate citizens. Were they buying from a company that helped protect the environment, paid workers fairly, and avoided child labor? Or were they paying discount prices because 12-year-olds were sewing their seams?

I dug up some dirt. Here are some of the cotton-pickin' problems with your product, JD:

- Cotton crops soak up almost a quarter of the world's insecticides each year. Blue jeans and other cotton clothes are creating some toxic issues.

- Each year, chemical manufacturers make thousands of tons of synthetic indigo, the dye used to color blue jeans. To create the dye, they use fuels such as oil or coal, and sometimes the process creates toxic by-products such as cyanide.

- Overseas factories can mean poor working conditions and even child labor. In Honduras, a woman sewing clothes for export might make $139 a month, and in parts of China, about $64. In Bangladesh, a similar worker makes just over $18 each month.

In 2003, a New York–based labor group brought a worker to Manhattan from a Honduran sweatshop. They staged a protest outside the store of a popular designer jeans maker, claiming that its jeans were made in sweatshops where workers were treated unfairly. People who had arrived to shop stayed outside on the sidewalk, listening as the 19-year-old girl described her factory, where workers were limited to two bathroom breaks a day and were forced to work overtime without pay. They weren't allowed to talk to each other in case they slowed down or tried to start a union. They were also regularly tested for pregnancy and HIV, and workers who tested positive were fired.

As the young woman continued to speak, reporters began to join the crowd of would-be shoppers. By the next day the worker's story had made newspaper headlines—and the company was rethinking the way it handed out contracts.

Jeans companies have spent almost two centuries advertising their products as symbols of freedom, individuality, and American liberty. Companies rely on advertising images of sexy models and free-spirited fun. Because of these images, jeans manufacturers are vulnerable to public opinion. It's hard for shoppers to feel sexy or free in their jeans after hearing about child labor or mistreated workers.

In 1991 Levi Strauss & Co. established a code of conduct requiring all contractors who produced their products to treat workers fairly. Company employees also began monitoring foreign factories, and Gap agreed to monitoring by independent reviewers. Guess Jeans launched a major anti-sweatshop campaign in 1997, labeling its clothing with tags that read: "This is a no-sweat garment."

Today, unions and non-profit organizations are working to educate shoppers. They encourage teens to read clothing labels and check company websites. More and more often, buyers are asking questions. Does the company supervise its contractors? Does it ban the use of child labor? Does it make unannounced visits to its factories to monitor safety standards? How does it deal with contractors that break the rules?

There are environmental considerations, too. Distressed jeans—with faded patches, worn seams, or irregular patterns in the dye—are a popular trend, but the processes used to make these jeans can be downright dangerous. According to some reports, the creeks around Mexican factories turn bright blue from the dye used. And workers may be exposed to toxic fumes from the acids and bleaches used in the distressing process. An organization called the Maquila Solidarity Network has been formed to draw attention to these issues and offer buyers information on how to buy "clean" jeans.

You won't find the answers to your questions on every company website. If you can't find the information you're looking for, try emailing or writing to the company's public relations department. When enough people write letters about their concerns, companies listen. After all, teens are these companies' biggest market. Indirectly, we control the blue jeans world!

Shoppers are asking more of their jeans than ever before. They want their pants to express both their politics and their personalities.

Ironically, the quest to wear something new and different has sometimes led shoppers to rediscover the past. In Japan there's a concept known as *wabi-sabi*—the idea that the value of something comes partly from its flaws. A favorite pair of jeans might have a missing belt loop and frayed seams, but they're completely comfortable. Their history has made the jeans even more precious.

After decades of exporting their ideas to other countries, jeans manufacturers took the Japanese *wabi-sabi* craze for vintage jeans home to North America. A former Levi's salesperson found an unworn, unwashed pair of decades-old jeans stuffed in the back of his dresser drawer. He sold them to a vintage clothing store for $2,500. When the store resold the pants, they received bids as high as $30,000. Even jeans memorabilia gained value. Buddy Lee dolls, the Lee brand mascot, have sold for hundreds of times what they originally cost.

Excuse me for a sec, while I run home and check the back of my closet!

It was obviously time for old to become new again. Or for new to become old. In 2002 a New Yorker named Troy Pierce was wearing his favorite pair of jeans to work, to ride his motorcycle, and even out to clubs at night. He rarely washed them. A Levi's jeans designer named Sun Choe happened to spot Troy in his tattered pants and immediately fell in love with them. She took the stained, smelly jeans back to her design team and used them as inspiration for a new look. Levi Strauss & Co. and other jeans companies such as Diesel and Ralph Lauren cashed in on the vintage market by making new, high-priced jeans from worn denim.

Other shoppers found different ways to personalize their pants. In August 1999, Levi Strauss & Co. opened a store in San Francisco where buyers could have their bodies scanned by beams of light that measured their waistline, their hips, and the length of their legs. Shoppers could design their ideal pants on a computer screen, and then the store would order them a custom-cut, perfectly fitted pair. By 2002 American Eagle was offering similar "customization stations," where shoppers could use stencils, razors, or pumice stones to individualize their purchases. From whiskered white creases on the thighs to lines of poetry in gold paint to intricate embroidery, jeans soon had every finishing detail imaginable.

A company called Fractal pioneered a process that used an industrial-size 2,500-watt laser to etch intricate patterns onto jeans. For a price, Fractal would even customize specific pairs with the buyer's signature or favorite patterns.

In the past decade, websites have sprung up to provide custom-made, personalized jeans orders. Citizens of Humanity jeans are said to be so exclusive, no two pairs are ever identical. Sweden's Nudie Jeans released a line of jeans meant to go unwashed for six months to a year, in order to develop a completely unique pattern of wear for each buyer. In 2011, a Canadian man made the news by wearing his pair for 15 months—unwashed. When they got smelly, he put them in the freezer for a while.

That would help cut down on my laundry!

So now there's every style imaginable—big and baggy, hip and trendy, skintight and sexy. There are going-camping-in-the-woods styles and heading-to-the-dance-club styles. Could people possibly need more jeans? Yes, yes, yes! At least, that's what the jeans companies need shoppers to believe. Billions of dollars depend on it. So how do you make people want your product? Show them that celebrities want it, too!

Companies have discovered that putting their pants on celebrity butts is a good way to get attention. Parasuco is a small Canadian company. In 2003, Salvatore Parasuco was convinced that the perfect spokesperson for his jeans would be young, rebellious rocker Avril Lavigne. Her first CD had just sold more than 14 million copies and she was idolized by teenage girls around the world.

But Avril wasn't likely to sign on as an advertising model—she was someone who wore what she liked and when she liked. Also, Parasuco didn't have an advertising budget large enough to tempt a rock star.

To catch Avril's attention, the company spent weeks studying her style and designing a pair of cargo pants just for her. They guessed at Avril's size, sent the pants to her manager, and waited for results.

Months went by, then suddenly Parasuco received a call from Avril's manager. The Canadian flag on the waistband of the cargo pants had caught Avril's eye, and she wanted to wear them to an awards show. When her manager provided the star's exact measurements, Parasuco whipped up a brand-new pair, happy to see them in front of a TV audience of 2.2 million.

Some companies, such as Wrangler, have had decades of practice using celebrities to endorse their jeans. Remember the rodeo stars and singing cowboys of the 1930s and '40s? In 2004 Wrangler hired NASCAR driver Dale Earnhardt Jr. to star in its magazine and TV ads, hoping to associate Earnhardt's energy and love for speed with "a new generation of Wrangler."

*R*ecently, some stars have used their fame to promote their own clothing ethics. British pop sensation Leona Lewis (called "the world's sexiest vegetarian" by PETA) is said to have spent hundreds of thousands of dollars on ethically produced clothing so she could promote it on her music tour. And U2's lead singer, Bono, launched his own eco-friendly fashion line in 2005.

Jeans have survived countless transformations, from work pants to army gear to play clothes and, eventually, school clothes. But they've never been as accepted as they are today. Business people sometimes wear them to work. The kids in the arcade and the skateboarders outside are all wearing them. Some churches even encourage their members to wear jeans, as a way of including people of every background and status level. Just as school uniforms make all students appear equal, jeans make all people appear equal. You can't tell the difference between a farmer and a politician when they're both wearing jeans.

*R*esearchers have suggested that we're actually happier wearing jeans. One study showed that when workers were allowed to wear casual clothes such as jeans to work, they called in sick less often. Scientists at the University of Wisconsin studied more than 50 workers who wore jeans to work on Fridays. They took an average of 491 more steps wearing jeans than they did in their dress clothes, and they burned an extra 25 calories a day. So not only did they put more energy into their jobs, they worked off some flab, too.

While jeans are for everyone, their subtle differences in style say something about people's personalities. Someone wearing the latest designer label is saying, "I keep up with fashion, I can afford the best, and appearances are important to me." The guy wearing a pair bought second-hand from the Salvation Army might be saying, "I can be cool without spending tons of money."

Mine say, "I'm comfortable when I'm boarding, and they're tough enough to take a fall."

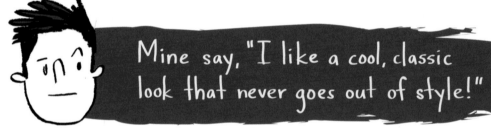

Mine say, "I like a cool, classic look that never goes out of style!"

There's no doubt that people love their jeans. The average American owns seven pairs, and Canadians hold on to almost as many. Jeans act as the perfect backdrop, the same way white walls in a gallery make the art stand out better. With a safe base of denim, we can try out a tube top or a bright cami or slip on a shaggy sweater. After more than 100 years, jeans continue to gain popularity, because for many of us a new pair is like a blank canvas, waiting for the imprint of our own personality.

FURTHER READING

Harris, Alice. *The Blue Jean*. New York: PowerHouse Books, 2002.

L'Hommedieu, John. *Changes: From Plant to Blue Jeans*. Chicago: Children's Press, 1998.

Olson, Nathan. *Levi Strauss and Blue Jeans*. Mankato: Capstone Press, 2007.

Sullivan, James. *Jeans*. New York: Gotham Books, 2006.

Weidt, Maryann N. *Mr. Blue Jeans: A Story about Levi Strauss*. Minneapolis: Lerner Publishing Group, 1992.

BIBLIOGRAPHY

"About LS & Co." Levi Strauss & Co. website, www.levistrauss.com/about.

"About the Gold Rush." Public Broadcasting System (PBS) website, www.pbs.org/goldrush/allabout.html.

Adkins, Jan. "The Evolution of Jeans," *Mother Earth News* (July/August 1990): p. 60.

American History: Lee Jeans 101. The Lee Company, 2000.

Barker, Olivia. "Nothing Comes Between Teens and Their Jeans—Not Even . . .," *USA Today* (September 5, 2002): p. 1D.

Barol, B., and E. A. Leonard. "Anatomy of a Fad," *Newsweek* (Summer/Fall 1990): p. 40.

"Blue Jean Workout," *Outside* (September 2004): p. 30.

Browne, Malcolm W. "Yugoslavs Foil Jeans Bootleggers," *New York Times* (March 20, 1977): p. 1.

"Clothes Made in Berlin Jail a Fashion Hit," AP Online (October 9, 2003), www.aponline/gov.in.

Douillard, André, and Jean-Marc St-Pierre, producers. *How It's Made* [video]. Filmwest Associates, 2001.

Goode, Stephen. "Blue-Jean Power," *Insight on the News* (August 16, 1999).

Gromer, Cliff. "Levi's Jeans," *Popular Mechanics* (May 1999): p. 94.

Harris, Carol. "Women under Fire in World War II." British Broadcasting Corporation (BBC) website, www.bbc.co.uk/history/war/wwtwo/women_at_war_03.shtml.

"Jeans—The Facts," *New Internationalist* (June 1998): p. 18.

Legan, Gary, producer. *The History of Blue Jeans* [video]. Estate Films Inc., 1995.

Lentz, Ellen. "East Germans Line up to Buy a Pair of Levi's," *New York Times* (November 30, 1978): p. D4.

O'Donnell, Jayne, and Michelle Walbaum. "Blue Jeans Selling Strong, but High-end Sales Could Suffer," *USA Today*, http://www.usatoday.com/money/industries/retail/2009-07-29-premium-jeans-sales_N.htm (accessed December 11, 2010).

"Our History." Lee Jeans website, www.leejeans.com/about_leejeans_history.asp.

Patoski, Joe Nick. "True Fit," *Texas Monthly* (September 1993): p. 120.

Philips, Alan. "$300 for Black-Market Jeans in Russia," *Globe and Mail* (December 3, 1979): p. 12.

Rodengen, Jeffrey L. *The Legend of VF Corporation*. Fort Lauderdale: Write Stuff Enterprises, 1998.

Schoenberger, Karl. *Levi's Children*. New York: Atlantic Monthly Press, 2000.

Scott, Sarah. "Inside Avril's Pants," *National Post Business* (September 2003): p. 52.

"The Shame of Sweatshops," *Consumer Reports* (August 1999): p. 18.

"Sweating for Fashion," *The Economist* (March 6, 2004): p. 14.

"The Teenagers," *Newsweek* (March 21, 1966): p. 57.

INDEX

101 Cowboy Pant 19

acid-washed jeans 77
advertising 21, 26, 28, 29–30, 40, 43, 50, 54, 58, 60, 74–75, 76, 90, 95, 99–100
American Civil Liberties Union 87
American Eagle 98
anarchists 63–64
Australia 65
Autry, Gene 30–31

Baker, Norma Jean see Monroe, Marilyn
Bardot, Brigitte 48
Belgium 65
bell-bottoms 55, 58, 60
Berlin 85
big band swing 32
Blue Bell 33, 40
Blue Denim 50
blues music 22
Bon Jovi 68
Bono 101
Brando, Marlon 44–45, 46
Brazil 65
Britain 35, 45, 50, 54, 65, 67
bumsters 87

California 5, 26; see also California gold rush; San Francisco
California gold rush 4, 5–8
Calvin Klein 74–75
Canada 35, 54, 71
Cassidy, Hopalong 30
Cavalli, Roberto 81
CBC Radio 35
Chicago 25
child labor 12–13, 93–94, 96
China 94
Choe, Sun 97
Churchill, Winston 67
Citizens of Humanity 98
Clash, The 63
Coca-Cola 71, 73
Combs, Sean (Diddy) 88
communism 66–70

Cornell University 27
cotton 7, 93, 94
coveralls 17, 37; see also Union-Alls; waist overalls
cowboys 21, 24–25, 29–31, 44, 77; see also dude ranches; rodeos
Croatia 71
Crosby, Bing 51
customized jeans 58, 63, 64, 98

Davis, Jacob 8–10
Dean, James 45, 46, 63, 85
Depression see Great Depression
designer labels 74, 79–81
destroyed jeans 78
Diamond, Neil 73
Diesel Jeans 90, 97
disco 60
distressed jeans 96
dude ranches 24
durability 5, 8, 19, 23, 26, 34; see also strength
Dussault, Jason 81
dye 94, 96

Earnhardt, Dale Jr. 100
East Germany 69
Eastern Oregon Correction Institution 83–84
England see Britain
environmental issues 94, 96
Europe 19, 48, 65, 71, 85, 87

factories 12, 16, 17, 35–37, 46, 51
    international 65, 71, 94, 96
    working conditions 12–13, 94, 96
    see also child labor; labor laws
farmers 17, 101
First World War 19
folk music 52
Fractal 98

Gap (clothing retailer) 96
Gentlemen Prefer Blondes 46
Germany 71
Girbaud, Marithe and François 76, 78
Givenchy 87

glam rock 73
Gloria Vanderbilt 74
gold rush *see* California gold rush
Great Depression 23–24, 26, 49
Gucci 81
Guess Jeans 96

Haeftling 85
H.D. Lee Mercantile Company 16; *see also*
    Lee Company; Lee Jeans
heavy metal music 73
hip hop 82, 83, 88
hip-huggers 57, 58
hippies 52, 55
Hollywood *see* movies
Honduras 94
Hong Kong 65
honky-tonk music 4
How to Marry a Millionaire 46
Hungary 69

Iron Curtain 67, 70; *see also* communism
Italy 77, 79

Japan 65, 71, 97
Jeanies 40
Jordache 74
Jou Jou 79

labor laws 13, 37; *see also* child labor; factories;
    working conditions
Latvia 8
Lauren, Ralph 77, 97
Lavigne, Avril 99
Lee Company 19, 20–21, 26, 60, 65, 97; *see*
    also H.D. Lee Mercantile Company; Lee,
    Henry David
Lee Frontier Lady Pants 40
Lee, Henry David 15–17
Lee Jeans 23, 26, 28, 40, 68, 71, 77; *see also* Lee
    Company
Lee Union-Alls 17, 19, 21
leisure suits 60
Levi Strauss & Co. 8, 10, 12–13, 15, 21, 26, 28,
    50–51, 60, 65, 69, 90, 96, 97, 98; *see also*
    Strauss, Levi
Levi's 23, 28, 43, 67, 68, 71
Lewis, Leona 101
London 63

Los Angeles 79
low-rise jeans 83, 86–88, 90

Maquila Solidarity Network 96
Marky Mark 75
Mavi Jeans 71
McCardell, Claire 39
McLuhan, Marshall 57
McQueen, Alexander 87
Mexico 96
Milan 79
Mods 59
Monroe, Marilyn 46, 73
Montreal 79
Moscow 66
movies 24, 30–31, 44–46, 48, 49, 50, 85
Murjani Corporation 74
music 4, 32, 48, 52, 58, 59, 63–65, 66, 68, 73, 74,
    82, 83, 85, 88, 90, 99, 101

Nevada silver rush 8
New Wave music 73
New York City 5, 25, 55, 63, 65, 79
Newsweek 54
Nudie Jeans 98

Obama, Barack 87
Oregon 83
overalls 16; *see also* waist overalls

Parasuco Jeans 79, 99
Parasuco, Salvatore 79, 99
Paris 65, 87
patents 10, 15
personalized jeans 58, 63, 64, 98
Philadelphia 30
Pierce, Troy 97
Pitt, Brad 90
pockets 8, 9, 16, 17, 19
politicians 101
preshrinking 17
Presley, Elvis 48, 85
Prison Blues 84
punk music 63–65

racism 37
Ramones, The 63
ranchers 24
rap 82, 83, 88

Rebel Without a Cause 45
recycling 7
Reno 8
Ripley's Believe It or Not! 26
rivets 9, 10, 12, 19, 21
rock and roll 48, 59, 66
Rockwell, Norman 36
Rodeo Ben 30, 41
rodeos 28, 29–30
Rogers, Roy 30
Rolling Stones 58, 73
Rosie the Riveter 37
Russia 67; *see also* USSR

saggin' 86–88
Salina, Kansas 15
Salk, Jonas 48
Salvation Army 102
San Francisco 5, 7, 8, 10, 55, 98
sandblasting 79
Saturday Evening Post 36
Schiffer, Claudia 75
Schram, Elton 26
Science Center of Ithaca 27
Scotland 65
seamstresses 11–13
Second World War 30, 32–39, 49, 65
    fabric shortages 33–34
    labor shortages 35–37, 46
    women in 35–37, 46
sex appeal 46, 48, 74–75, 76, 95
Sex Pistols 65
Shields, Brooke 74
shrinking 17, 43; *see also* preshrinking
Sid Vicious 65
Simmons, Russell 88
Smithsonian Institute 53
smuggling 67, 69, 83
Sonny and Cher 58
Spain 65, 71
Spears, Britney 90
Springsteen, Bruce 74
Stern, Louis 13
stonewashing 77
Strauss, Abraham 13
Strauss, Jacob 13
Strauss, Levi 5, 7, 10, 13
Strauss, Sigmund 13
strength 26, 27; *see also* durability

suspenders 11, 19, 21
swing music *see* big band swing

t-barring 88
teenagers 43, 50–51, 53–55
    economic power 54, 79, 96
    teen rebellion 45, 49, 57, 62, 63, 77
Tegel Prison 85
Turkey 71
Twisted Sister 68

U2 101
uniforms 18, 19, 33–34, 35, 83; *see also* First
    World War; Second World War
Union-Alls 17
United States 50, 65, 77, 86
University of Wisconsin 101
U.S. Army 33, 51
USSR 48, 66, 68–69

Vanderbilt, Gloria 74
Vermont 15
Victoria's Secret 75
Vietnam War 56
vintage jeans 97
Vogue 25

wabi-sabi 97
waist overalls 10
Warhol, Andy 73–74
Wayne, John 25
Wild One, The 44–45
Wild West 4, 5, 24–25, 28, 31, 57, 77; *see also*
    cowboys; ranchers
Wolf, Brigadier General Leonard 19
women
    and jean design 17, 40–41
    in wartime 18, 35–37, 46
    workers 11–14, 35–37
Woodstock 57
working conditions 12–13, 93–94, 96; *see also*
    child labor; factories; labor laws
Wrangler Jeans 28–30, 33, 41, 43, 54, 65, 68, 71,
    100; *see also* Blue Bell

Yugoslavia 67

zippers 11, 20–21, 40, 41